SHADES
Nuancing Listening Prayer

Sean Davidson
and Brad Jersak

The material herein was first developed on Agora, a newsgroup based at Briercrest College and Seminary, and was first published as an article at *www.clarion-journal.ca* in August 2006.

Printed in Altona, MB Canada by Friesens Book Division.

Cover design: Stephen "Jonny Chance" Jersak
Cover art: "Image: 3d glasses.jpg" used by permission from Wikimedia Commons (http://sxc.hu/browse.phtml?f=view&id=293332).

Library and Archives Canada Cataloguing in Publication

Jersak, Brad, 1964-

Shades : nuancing listening prayer / Brad Jersak, Sean Davidson.

ISBN 0-9780174-3-9 (pbk.)

1. Prayer--Christianity. 2. Listening--Religious aspects--Christianity. 3. Spiritual life--Christianity. 4. Jersak, Brad, 1964-
Can you hear me? : tuning in to the God who speaks.
 I. Davidson, Sean, 1971- II. Title.

BV4817.J47 2006   248.3   C2006-905160-7

Fresh Wind Press
2170 Maywood Ct.
Abbotsford, B.C.
Canada V2S 4Z1

www.freshwindpress.com

SHADES
Nuancing Listening Prayer

Sean Davidson
and Brad Jersak

with Sam Berg, Dwight Friesen,
Kevin Hall, Andre Harden, David Miller,
Glenn Runnalls, and Colleen Taylor

Fresh Wind Press

Foreword
Glenn Runnalls

I've known Brad Jersak for some twenty years and Sean for a little over half that time. Brad and Sean were introduced to each other in the context of a newsgroup called Agora. It formed out of an ongoing email conversation between some grads and faculty of a Christian College on the Canadian Prairies. Over the years, this newsgroup has explored a number of recurring themes, sometimes going in circles, sometimes making headway, always concerned for learning from each other for the sake of knowing Jesus better.

After Sean Davidson graduated from the Christian College in Saskatchewan, he returned to Ontario for continuing education. Transferring into a Public University, he graduated at the top of his class. Sean finished his Masters Degree and then started his PhD studies. It was during this time Sean joined Agora. Intense, forthright, articulate, always seeking truth, desiring to find and follow Jesus, Sean brought a unique style to Agora and together we all learned what it means for iron to sharpen iron. Probably more than any other current members of Agora, Sean and Brad are continuously used by Jesus to show each other his way.

Not surprisingly, with Brad's involvement, "Listening Prayer" has been one of the recurring themes of Agora. Brad's invitation to "Listening Prayer" is an invitation to take the personal presence of God seriously, to explore what it means to be in conversation with a God who is alive, a God who is here, a God who speaks to His children, not only in the Scriptures and in sermons, but in the context of prayer.

I have had three main interests in Listening Prayer. The first, was in helping my students to let the Lord set direction in their daily living. This was especially important for me in evangelism... I found that the practical deism of modernist evangelicalism had led to two unhealthy approaches. The first was some variation of the gospel gunslinger—the guy who's always looking for another notch in his gun... the gospel was reduced to a sales pitch ready to be used on any hitchhiker or stranger on any bus or plane (funny how you had to trap some-one in a conveyance). The second unhealthy approach was a reactive contempt for words. Usually it would involve some variation of "Preach the Gospel always and when necessary, use words." Neither of these approaches with their rules for evangelism seemed to reflect the Great Commission or the experiences shown us in Acts. I had experienced significant fruitfulness in evangelism under the Lord's direction and I heard similar testimony of others. But when students asked, "How do you know it is the Lord directing you?" the answer, "Hear and obey," was never enough. How do you teach a group of young people who have been raised as practical de-ists to tune into the Spirit of the Lord? ... along came Brad.

The other interest I had was for those students who were bound by fear and darkness. They could say all the right things to do and think, but somehow they were overcome by lies. Brad bore testimony that he was seeing the Lord speak into people's lives in a way that the power of lies was being

5

broken. Brad taught a set of expectations and practices that would help people who wanted to be free of lies and fears to listen to the Lord so that He would set them free. The fruit of this has been amazing.

The third aspect of learning Listening Prayer with Brad has been the way in which it has impacted my ongoing relationship with Jesus. Listening Prayer isn't just about direction and freedom. It is ultimately about worshipping a God who is here and who is not silent. Yes, there is much good fruit that comes from following the direction of the Lord and from finding the freedom that he has for us, but the most important thing is the fellowship that he desires for us. It is wonderful to find out that he is not only our Counsellor and our Comforter but also our Confidant.

Over the last couple of years, I have encountered many people who have benefited significantly from Brad's foundational work on Listening Prayer, *Can You Hear Me?* (2003). His books, teaching and ministry have given many who are anxious, fearful, and self-doubting the confidence to trust the living God of the Scriptures more fully. Many people were led to discover healing and wholeness in Jesus. At the same time, there are not a few detractors. Many of these detractors would like to make Brad accountable to themselves. Instead, Brad continually submits himself and his teaching to the Lord through select groups of discerners who test and weigh his teaching and ministry. Brad's home church is one such group. Agora functions as another. The discussion that follows reflects an important round in the process of testing and weighing what it means to listen to the Lord in prayer.

SHADES
Nuancing Listening Prayer

In July and August, 2006, nine members of Agora, a newsgroup and think-tank based in Canada, engaged in a discussion around the topic of hearing God's voice. The trigger point was an article by John Blake in The Atlanta Journal-Constitution but the focus turned quickly to "Listening Prayer" as described in Brad Jersak's book, **Can You Hear Me?**

As we dialogued, the simultaneous resisting and affirming became very productive. The effect of bringing together our various "lenses" was reminiscent of 3D glasses in which the combination of different shades and points of view revealed a depth of vision not possible to any one person.

The main dialogue occurred between Sean Davidson and Brad Jersak, while seven others from Agora piped up at important junctures.

David:

There's an interesting article here:
http://www.ajc.com/search/content/living/stories/
0708Reltalk.html

Hearing from God: Some spiritual leaders claim to be on speaking terms with the Almighty.

By JOHN BLAKE <mailto:jblake@ajc.com>
The Atlanta Journal-Constitution
Published on: 07/08/06

"God told me..."

The Bible says God speaks in a "still, small voice," but that voice no longer seems to be still or small if you listen to contemporary pastors. The phrase "God told me" is becoming one of their favorite expressions. So many seem to be on speaking terms with God.

Turn on the TV or the radio, and one will inevitably encounter a preacher flashing what one pastor calls the "God trump card." It signals that the holder is the recipient of a steady stream of revelations from God on matters big and small.

It's invoked so often that few question it, but two recent examples stand out... [for the rest of the article, follow the link above].

Brad:

The only thing more terrifying than pastors who claim God speaks to them are pastors who know he doesn't. We really must hear this article. However, Blake's cynicism does not begin to solve the problem. The solution to pastors who falsely claim to hear God is not a cessation of listening. We need to listen better rather than shutting our ears. The fruit of listening together is REALLY good: healing, community, tremendous safety. The counterfeit abounds, not just to seduce us into hearing the wrong voices, but to cause us to plug our ears.

One more thing: God is much much closer than our cell phone.

Sean:

... and at the same time (paradoxically) he is also much farther away than the telegraph.

I agree that a corrective is needed. That there are counterfeits means that we require a model of healthy listening. With you. But part of healthy listening means that we resist the demand for immediate answers.

As David pointed out to me a while ago, we keep circling around God's imminence/transcendence in our conversations. Here's the thing: we do not listen because God is fully imminent. Nor do we plug up our ears because he is fully transcendent. We pray confidently and unceasingly with listening hearts, attending to the living God who is very near and very far and trusting him implicitly as we allow him to answer in his own way, according to his own timing.

Brad:

Yeah. That's good. And yet... do you see the difference between expectancy based on promise versus the demand when God decides to play it his way? I mean, I don't think my expectation that he'll answer when I call (e.g. Jeremiah 33:3) should be regarded as a demand.

Sean:

I hear you. At this point, I'm comfortable with "expectancy based on promise" if we are to understand such expectancy in terms of a living hope rather than something bordering on unconditional necessity. The qualifier "immediate" is important here. God has promised to answer, but not precisely here, at this time, in this way, for this purpose, etc.

It's often the case that we set the parameters for God in the way that we understand his promises and expect to hear from him. And so there's this impulse to move from "God promised this" to a strong, definitive "therefore" that would serve to determine not only the what, but also the when/where/how/why. When we make this subtle shift in our hearts, we're no longer listening. We are presuming.

So an "expectation that he'll answer when I call" could very easily take on the nature of a demand if we begin to presume the precise conditions of the answer. In a case like this, the very motive for listening (i.e. God's promises) can end up serving the purposes of idolatry. Here's the difference between expectancy-hope and expectation-demand: the former looks to the living God to come and watches/waits for his coming while the latter erects a god on top of promises that are treated as formulae, a god that looks remarkably like a vending machine.

Brad:

Yes, I like what you are saying concerning "a living hope" and the "immediate" qualifier.

The thing is, I don't meet very many people who expect to hear from God. Most tell me all the reasons they can't. They have already been told they can't or intimidated by elitists who do or think they would if they were worthy. They are absolutely frustrated. In real world *churchianity*, there is still a famine of hearing. But when they do start to believe that God speaks, the parameters and expectations they develop do often enter just as you said, and these only further confirm in their own minds that they can't hear, because God doesn't play by our rules most of the time. That's why I try to break open their narrow parameters and say, "God speaks in many ways. You just aren't counting them... and most of them are not as weird OR as narrow as you think."

I'm trying to understand the idolatry aspect... it feels like I am missing something.

Concerning the vending machine analogy, I've seen this problem from time to time. But then there's the model John uses in Revelation 3. If someone is already knocking at the door, is it really that presumptuous to expect someone to be at the door when you open it? That's the biblical model... an expectation created by Jesus for the purpose of fellowship.

On the other hand, and in agreement with you, if I am knocking on the door, (as per Jesus' parables on prayer), he does promise to answer but he does not say when or how. Yet he actually encourages us to persist and even nag and call him down from bed. It looks like he's encouraging us to presume. His statements on prayer seem like less of a humble posture than you and I would counsel.

The word that Jesus uses for both the above realities—opening the door to expect a visitor or knocking on the door to expect an answer—is faith, not presumption. Maybe where presumption comes is in our response to the mystery of why the door is not answering or why the knocker is gone (cf. Song of Songs)... if we become accusers of God.

All that to say, I don't remember Jesus ever rebuking someone for expecting something more than he offered... except his mother, and then he did it anyway... our problem is not usually that we expect too much, but far too little. When Ahaz uses fear of presumption as a case for his unwillingness to ask for a sign, God was quite upset with him. The question was almost, "who are you NOT to presume?"

Don't get me wrong, I'm more comfortable with the humble waiting, surrender to mystery, quietly hunkering down as God does his God thing. But in so doing, I see that I may be trying to be more like Jesus than Jesus and more biblical than the Bible. This too is a tension.

Sean:

There's a lot here to mull over. Listening...

I'm thinking about the nature of the corrective.

Widening the parameters to include the many ways that God speaks is one really important way of remedying abuse. With you. Here are a few others: It's okay to listen and be met with silence for a season. It's okay to ask and receive something other than what you expected. It's okay to cry out with urgent questions and not to be answered right away. The important thing, as in any significant relationship, is to keep listening, asking, and crying out. The silence and surprising turns do not indicate a lack of care on God's part. Nor do they suggest that we're somehow less than worthy or ill-equipped.

We need "double-vision" to see the possibility for idolatry in Listening Prayer. Hopeful expectancy is never a purely simple thing. It can so easily modulate into demanding expectation and this is because of the deceitfulness of the heart (Jeremiah 17:9). It seems to me that we all look to God expectantly (especially in times of extreme suffering and crisis) and this is a good thing. Augustine is right, our hearts do not find rest until they rest in God. We know this intuitively. It's how we're wired. Now it's true that our confidence can grow as we become aware of God's promises and begin to treat them seriously, but this same confidence can turn to presumption quite easily, especially when we believe from the outset that we're immune to going astray. With a kind of adolescent impatience we can come to focus narrowly and almost *"scientistically"* on the promises rather than continuing to engage the living God who made them. At a certain point we stop listening and asking. Having shut our ears and closed our eyes, we turn the promises into predictable formulae and begin expecting "god" to do things according to our understanding of the situations/circumstances in our lives even as we believe that we're simply taking the living God at his word.

It's strange but true: we can end up adopting a posture of subtle accusation even when we believe that we're being most faithful. Unfortunately, this tends to escape us at first. Insofar as our presumption is sustainable and the "stubborn fact" of God's otherness has not come to bear, we can easily feel like we're tracking with the living God when in actual fact we are subtlety at war with him and are in the process of erecting a god more to our liking.

When we finally come to realize all of this, often at the point that God breaks in and frustrates our expectations, the disillusionment can be significant (I'll bet that many of us who've lacked the confidence to listen to God do so because of past missteps rather than lack of attempts).

It's easy to become a functional if not confessing cessation-ist when we've come to a recognition of our own propensity to idolatry. Then again, we may lack this recognition and like Blake's prophet-pastors plow ahead either unaware or unconcerned or confidently self-deceived. In extreme cases, we can force our agenda and begin to declare "Thus saith the Lord" at all points where our ego has gained a sense of mastery.

Thinking about how this relates to self-deception: I'm not sure that asking *"Was that just me?"* in conversation with God needs to "reinforce independence, introduce doubt, and end the conversation immediately" (*Can You Hear Me?* 92). It's a helpful question given our tendency to fashion a god in our own image. The conversation can continue and even become more rich, but we must tune our ears to counterpoint (as in music) and train our eyes to see double.

Paradoxically, the question can help us to step outside our-selves and our narrow view of things, rather than merely re-inforcing them. That is, it can help us in the process of con-versation to "examine what we consider to be plain verities about [the Other],... to entertain the idea that these 'verities' may be so many ugly prejudices, bitter fruits of our imagi-nary fears or our sinister desires to dominate or exclude.

We [can] also observe our own images of ourselves... [and] detect layers of self-deceit that tell us exalted stories about ourselves" (Volf, *Exclusion and Embrace,* 251). On the other hand, it can help prepare us for appreciating the strangeness of the Other. In distancing ourselves for a moment by asking "Was that just me?" we are not necessarily introducing doubt. We're also making "ready for a surprise" (252). Such distancing prepares us to "open our ears to hear how [God] perceives [Himself] as well as how [He] perceive[s] us."

Colleen:

As I read *Can You Hear Me?* I see that Brad does encourage questioning, but prefers to question Jesus (i.e. "Was that you?") rather than the self.

Given the inherent deceitfulness of the human heart, it seems that both questions can be problematic.

Sean:

Yes, I hear you. There's no silver bullet.

Here's the thing: "Was that me?" need not compete with "Was that you?" The response to either can come from myself, the Other or a chiming combination of both, but whatever it is that comes out will require testing and weighing.

The important thing here is the double vision...

When we listen it is healthy to have an ear not only for the voice of the Spirit, but also our own. At times, they will coincide. At others, there will be significant discord and when this happens it will not always be easy to distinguish between my speaking "I" and the voice of "Thou." It'll also take time to notice exactly how we've gone astray and what a return to the living God might entail. The significant thing though is that we actually get the discord. This is precisely what the rich young ruler experienced. He went away sad because Jesus' response failed to chime with the voice of his heart telling him that perfect rule-keeping was sufficient. It's good that he got the discord rather than either excluding Jesus' voice outright or craftily assimilating it to his own. When there's discord, we can stop and rest for a while, knowing that something's up. It's okay.

Throughout we've got the promise of hearing the voice of the Good Shepherd, so we need not fret if we're a little off track. We need to keep coming back to listen and ask and call out. We need to invite others to come alongside and listen with us. We need to read the Scriptures and get our charismatic exercise in the community of faith. Jesus promises us that we will in fact hear his voice in such a way that enables us to walk in truth and love.

Brad, what do you think of Volf's concept of double vision in relation to Listening Prayer? At least in the way that I've spelled it out...

Here's the reason for double vision:

1) we have good reason to distrust the motives of our hearts;
2) we have good reason to entrust ourselves fully to God.

Brad:

Thanks for filling things out a little concerning idolatry.

I agree with your use of the "Was that just me?" question and I like the connection to Volf. I think we need to listen to both God's voice and our own hearts in conversation. "Was that just me?" only becomes unhealthy when its function is to end dialogue and when its source is *not* my heart, but rather, the accuser implying that it's ALWAYS just me so that I may as well stop listening.

Can you hear me? would have probably been better if we'd co-written it. Bear in mind that my primary target audience were functional cessationists. I was making the point: "God speaks. Tune in." And I was trying to remove blocks to those who want to hear but can't. So again, "Was that just me?" is not automatically a bad question as long as it's a genuine question in pursuit of an answer. But as I've encountered it (let's say 2000 times conservatively), it's usually a rhetorical question meaning, "It's always just me? I never hear."

Glenn:

Really good stuff...

Testing and weighing is also about, "I know that was you Lord. This is what I heard; did I get it right?"

I've continued to reflect on this, partly because we've been talking about it at Gathering leadership. Testing and weighing is *not mainly* about identifying the sound of God's voice... tuning in to the signal...

It only takes a couple of calls from a loved one on your cell phone to be able to recognize her/his voice. There will be times when the reception is so bad that you may have to ask, "Is that you?" But you don't need full signal strength or perfect fidelity to be able to know the caller is your friend/wife/husband/child.

Testing and weighing is the same as in most conversations. It's about other things... "Am I hearing you right; am I getting your meaning?" And this is where we come back to transcendence.

How many stories are there about children (and others) who hear the wrong words in Christmas Carols? Why Christmas Carols? It's the transcendence, the otherness of their subject.

God speaks to us and we keep imposing/projecting on his transcendence; we domesticate him. We do this both in our rationalizing and theologizing as well as in the immediate apprehension of his voice.

So we have to test: "Lord, is this what you were saying? Is this what you meant?"

There's a third aspect to testing and weighing that is cyclical... and it flies in the face of our linear/eye orientation...

One of the reasons that some folk have a hard time buying what you are teaching, Brad, is because they are afraid of finality...

Linear/eye-oriented reading moves from beginning to end and the conclusion is final. Seeing makes us more solipsistic. When we are naively oriented toward the eye, we conflate our understanding with reality itself. Besides the brain mechanics of seeing versus hearing, there is the very process of reading that is quite different in mechanics from hearing—I'm speaking of normal functions here— we don't read on the periphery... we hear all around us...

Once we've been taught to read the squiggles we "get them"—it's "black and white." Unless we're wearing headphones, hearing is always a matter of filtering out one set of sounds from another set of sounds.

Given a familiarity with the subject and decent spelling, we know what each word is and means almost simultaneously with seeing it. We may have to wait for the end of a clause or sentence to hear what was being said and meant by a particular word.

Here's what I see around here (at Briercrest College and Seminary):

Students are looking for final answers. They are trying to obtain "the mind of Christ" which is synonymous for them with absolute truth/final certainty.

It doesn't take them long to realize that Briercrest profs do not collectively have the mind of Christ... There is no line to follow and if there's any harmony, they haven't been trained to hear it.

So then they assume they can find the mind of Christ by going to some particular guru (on or off campus), study of the original languages (Greek especially... *"What? Jesus spoke Aramaic????!!!"*), or pursue logic/theology.

And then along comes guru Brad...

You don't need all that hard work to have the mind of Christ... He has sent us his Spirit... and if you are his sheep, you will hear his voice.

And the linear/print oriented folk (naive and otherwise) impose a kind of finality that Brad didn't (shouldn't) intend.

And I return to the cyclical. Hearing is never final... there are no punctuation marks. Even when we leave, there is, "until we meet again."

Training in vowel oriented literacy leads us to a delusion of equating understanding with constant progress... a > b > c.

Peter hears and understands that Jesus was the Messiah, the Son of God. Which leads him to conclude that he will not lose in his battle against the Romans... which means he doesn't get what Jesus is saying about the coming Passion. And so, "Get behind me Satan."

Did Peter ever get what Jesus wanted with the Gentiles? Yes. Did Peter always get what Jesus wanted with the Gentiles? No. He had to be reminded over and over again...

And this is something else that people don't get about your teaching. Hearing "directly" from the Spirit does not privilege our understanding anymore than it did Peter's. The Epistles of Paul and Peter are finally authoritative, but not because Paul and Peter were perfect in their understanding of what they heard/read/said/wrote.

The mind of Christ involves abiding, abounding... again, it's cyclical. Of course by saying it is cyclical, I am saying it is conversational...

But it is more than conversational. It's a dance... but not the perichoresis of the Trinity... it's more like a father with his five-year-old daughter.

Sometimes the dance is a waltz with God sweeping me up into his arms and carrying me along. Sometimes he is bending over almost breaking his back so that I can feel all grown-up because I'm almost leading. Sometimes it is a waltz with me stepping on his toes. Sometimes I'm keeping in step, but that's because I'm being carried along on his big feet. Sometimes in the dance, I am sitting down, exhausted, and watching him carry on as if I were still there.

Mostly the dance is me just shaking my jiggles out and him standing back and grooving along, clapping...

Brad:

Wow. Continuing conversation rather than the final word. Ceaseless dance versus a final stand or stance.

Glenn:

But using the analogy of testing and weighing, we must remember that we test and weigh for truth/goodness/beauty. We are looking for the precious metal/stones...

Sean:

... rather than the combustibles.

Glenn:

Most of my above post was about testing/weighing as reinforcing confidence.... There is a testing and weighing in the context of "doubt" (note the prospecting analogy in italics):

"I'm not sure that was the Lord because I haven't been tuning in much lately."

> *I've seen way too much mica and haven't seen a lot of gold in a long while.*

"I'm not sure that was the Lord because I'm in a place in my life where the signal is weak."

> *I know there's something there... but it's buried way deep.*

"I'm not sure that was the Lord because there's a lying Spirit."

Someone's trying to get me to buy their mine.

"I'm not sure that was the Lord because I've realized that I've fallen into the temptation of building my kingdom and I've conflated 'I' and 'Thou'."

I've developed a taste for chromed plastic and glass baubles.

"I'm not sure that was the Lord because he's speaking with an unfamiliar voice."

You are not supposed to find gold here!

There's also a doubting that happens when what is being said is out of this world:

"That's crazy!? Is that what you really said? You mean this? But what about..."

What? You want me to sell all I have and buy this land to look for buried treasure? Doesn't it say, "a bird in the hand is worth two in the bush"?

By the way, there are all kinds of prospectors, but most of them look for gold where they know the gold is—Scripture, God's people, God's Spirit within me.

Brad:

This is gold, Glenn.

Sean, there's something niggling away at me a little. Can we back up a bit? You had said that God is also "much farther away than the telegraph." I think it'd probably be helpful for you to know that I no longer equate transcendence with "far." Following Jenson, the transcendence of God is found in, not behind or beyond, Christ. The most inaccessible mysteries of God are all contained within the heart and the mind of the One we know intimately and who lives in us. So the transcendence of God is about mining the depths of relationship within rather than an out of bounds zone beyond the blue.

It's not a contradiction to say, "I know the Transcendent One" because his mysteries are not something apart from his person and his person is with us always. It just means, I don't and won't know all the depths of this person who has wooed me. To put it a different way that honors "farther away" language, I now live on and swim in the ocean of God. I know the ocean. I never leave the ocean. The ocean is around me and within me all the time. But admittedly, I've never seen the bottom of the ocean or the farthest shores of the ocean. In that sense, there is a sense of distance. "Unfathomable" is a nautical term from depth beyond measuring. But I'm in the midst of it all.

Yes, we need to resist the counterfeits and we need to replace them with a model of healthy listening, but I think we need to be far more open and forthright with this. We need more rather than less listening. Healthy listening will include new strengths of discernment that move us past, "You guys aren't really hearing" and on to, "Thus says the Lord, 'You guys aren't hearing! And here is why. And here is what he's saying." Blake uses a worst-of list to create cynicism. That's not God's voice either.

And yet... and yet I can't help but hear God's grief in it. His indignation. In some ways, Blake echoes Jeremiah and others, but he doesn't quite get to chapter 31. Jeremiah's solution to "the prophets are liars" ends up being a surprising, "You will all know me, from the least to the greatest."

Resist immediate answers? Yes and no. If I'm hearing the spirit of what you say, I have to agree. Easy, pithy, banal answers? Sure, resist them. Untested, unweighed, unaccountable words from leaders with an agenda? Absolutely, wave a red flag. But let's not stray too far from the promises of God that are now "yes" and "amen" in Jesus:

> For example, Isaiah 58:8-9:
>> *Then your light will break forth like the dawn,*
>> *and your healing will quickly appear;*
>> [speaks of a quick answer]
>> *then your righteousness will go before you,*
>> *and the glory of the LORD will be your rear guard.*
>> [speaks of his constant nearness]
>> *Then you will call, and the LORD will answer;*
>> *you will cry for help, and he will say: Here am I.*
>> [implies immediate response]

I see this a fair bit in Scripture... answers before you hardly ask, conversations that don't involve waiting around but rather, tit for tat. It's just there, regardless of the asses that claim it vainly. It's also just how it works in the Listening Prayer contexts that lead to true and dramatic healing. I don't see that resistance would be necessary, preferable or even appropriate in those cases. Often, resistance to God's immediate voice in those settings is regarded as unbelief or faithlessness.

Again, concerning transcendence, I think Jenson is the guy. Yancey also did some work on this. His emphasis is on Christ's offensive on the Jewish doctrine of transcendence, summarized in his use of "Abba." I think that's in *The Jesus I Never Knew*. I don't think he has the corner on the topic, but he warns us not to be on the wrong side of Jesus in the immanence/transcendence debates. We'd best not side with the priesthood who extended distance while Christ was collapsing it. Still, I think Jenson is wiser here.

Sean:

Hmm. I trust you but I find myself resisting...

I'm having trouble with your conception of transcendence. I can see how the indwelling of the Spirit in the heart does not negate divine transcendence, but I'm not sure that divine transcendence should be defined in terms of an all-encompassing heart. Indeed, transcendence suggests incomprehensibility, not unknowability. With you. And yet it also suggests what Rudolf Otto termed the *mysterium tremendum*.

Concerning Isaiah 58:8-9, I would want to understand this according to the familar tension in Scripture between the "now" and "not yet." What the passage describes is a reality that is emerging, to be sure, and it begins with Jesus and the coming of the Spirit. But I'm not sure that we should be living as though it has come to complete fruition. And so, we continue to listen and ask and call out, but we do not live at the point of full arrival and so in addition to hearing and obeying there's waiting and wondering and expostulating and testing, etc.

I'm wondering what you mean by "the imminence/transcendence debates." Does this distinction set the conditions for a debate? Isn't it a paradox that we must continually affirm rather than a contradiction that we seek finally to overcome?

A little further on you say that Jesus collapses the distance between ourselves and God... Hmm. I don't think I'm comfortable with this notion. Why would we feel a need to choose between a priestly expansion of distance and a Christly collapsing of distance.

Here's the thing: Whatever transcendence means it's not what the priestly guardians take it to mean (i.e. impersonal distance mediated by a select few). As a result, I don't think we should be understanding imminence as the opposite of this false notion of transcendence.

Brad:

I'm not intending to define transcendence in terms of the

human heart. I'm saying that all the mysteries and transcendence of God are in Christ in that he is God, the fullness of the measure of God, who now knows all the mysteries of God, and expresses fully the character of God. And this Christ, while not "contained" by any one of us, is nevertheless "fully present" in all of us who are in him and known (though only in part, intimately and personally) to us whom he now calls friends. The key here is that transcendence is not an ethereal unknown of some essence, but rather, a personal trait of a living God who has made himself known. Here's where Jenson makes sense to me [you may want to read the broader context: Robert Jenson, *What if it were true?* Reflections CTI, Vol. 4 Spring 2001, 13-14]:

God does not know and intend himself as a divine essence, but as a particular, a specific someone, and indeed as someone whom we also know, and indeed as the man of the Gospels and the prophets, the man of sorrows acquainted with grief, the proclaimer of the Kingdom in which the last will be first and the first last, the friend of publicans and sinners, the enemy and participant of human suffering, Mary's boy and the man on the cross. We can to a limited extent abstract the conception of a divine essence, of divinity as such, and this conception will be comprised of such predicates as "impassible," "omnipotent," "omniscient," and the rest of them. But God does not, if Jesus is the Logos, first know himself as an essence. Also for God, insofar as he knows himself this way, such knowing is a secondary abstraction.

Indeed, we do not live at the point of fruition. This makes sense especially in the narrative of Scripture and in our lives... yours and mine. The two sides represented in the article in either extreme: to the one, God will never talk; to the other, God will never wait. So "full arrival"? Of course not. We see and presumably hear as in a mirror dimly. We wait and wonder and hold our breath. This is so true to life—even to Paul's life and the first apostles.

Yet even a theologically respectable tension does tend to buckle under the strength of Jesus' words in John 16. We mustn't be more reasonable than the Master who "bragged" about the coming infusion: "all that the Father has is mine"; "whatever the Spirit hears, he will make known to you" and "guide you into all truth." Shockingly, these promises SHOULD give rise to the expectations of the foolish preachers that the Blake cited—which is why I tend to battle them, not with a call for less revelation, but MORE. And this more includes a broader and thicker range of testing. Discernment is not a function of limiting the voice of God... it IS a category of the voice of God.

Re: the "imminence/transcendence debates"... I'm referring mainly to the differences among the old mystics concerning apophatic and kataphatic theology (e.g. the contrast between the intimacy of the Spanish Carmelites versus Pseudo-Dionysius and later, the author of the *Cloud of Unknowing*). But also, the practical use of a theology of transcendence that would say, "Who are you to say that God answers when you call?" In other words, the problem is not transcendence itself, but a misuse of the theology to negate revelation. You say, "whatever transcendence means it's not what the priestly guardians take it to mean (i.e. impersonal distance mediated only by a select few)."

This is very helpful. Maybe I need to hear you define transcendence again more clearly—perhaps a little list of what it is and what it isn't. It seems like I'm battling with the definitions of others who misuse the term rather than engaging with your probably more orthodox version. However, what I am fairly sure about (by that I mean, I'm sure that I mean this, not I'm sure that I'm right) is that the issue of transcendence can be confused or clarified around the analogies of location that we use. When I think of immanence and transcendence as "close" and "far away" simultaneously, that doesn't look like paradox. It's a simple contradiction. In fact, the similarity of the words makes them sound as if they are in like categories, which they are not. Let me explain:

When I think of imminence, I hear "nearness" (he is always near according to Matthew 28 and many other texts, always with us according to Psalm 139, etc., never leaving us, never forsaking us).

I do not think it follows that transcendence as "not-nearness," but rather, the mysterious nature and unknowable or at least ineffable aspects of this very-near-One. I can't control or contain him in my categories, nor even in words like transcendence... whatever transcendence is (*mysterium tremendum*, absolute otherness, and so on), it is not so much

31

about where God is or even how frequently or immediately he speaks, but about who he is in this dynamic friendship. It is only in relationship that we discover that he is untamable; his ways are not our ways and his thoughts are incomprehensible (i.e. transcendence is known existentially from an unfathomable encounter rather than an non-encounter). This even applies to his silence. While I may pray, "where did you go?", the real question is why I'm not "feeling" or "hearing" or "seeing" someone so close with whom certain covenants tell me I should expect otherwise. And that's a mystery.

Glenn:

Brad, I love it when you do theology...

Brad:

I remember you saying that before. Thanks for encouraging us/me. Sean and David continually help me along with it. I'm curious about what you're seeing or what happens when you see it?

Glenn:

There's a persistence... in pursuing Jesus and hearing/ speaking truth... that results in these wonderful turns... and I get these "aha's" that are simultaneously akin to having a friend put me on to a missing word in a crossword puzzle and a childish delight in a visit from grandma...

Brad:

Wow, do I ever relate to the crossword analogy. Can you point out the "aha" that came this time?

Glenn:

Particularly around imminence and transcendence... that they aren't actually logical opposites. And then in general the way in which you were calling us to 1) heed Jesus of the Gospels; 2) meet Jesus in the now.

Brad:

Right. So God is imminent (which is about his nearness) and God is transcendent (which is about his otherness). Nearness and otherness aren't opposites. In fact, the former confirms and amplifies the latter. Nor does transcendence and otherness have to deny intimacy or even union. What it will do is ensure that intimacy and union are transformative. When you get close to the consuming fire, you are refined.

But also, as it pertains to the Listening Prayer discussion, transcendence is irrelevant to the possibility of intimate conversation, (that is, it does not deny the possibility and reality of a friend-to-friend conversation with the transcendent one) and always has been, from Eden to Abraham to Jacob to Moses to Joshua to David and so on.

It does mean that there are other conversations besides the intimate ones. There are the types where you think you might die. Why, on one day, do I feel like my prayer time is like pillow-talk, and on another occasion, I may need to wear Depends? Certainly God is not less imminent or transcendent on either day. He's just giving me a different revelation of himself, I suppose.

Glenn, you mentioned my call to "1) heed Jesus of the Gospels; 2) meet Jesus in the now."

Yes! These are passions of mine. In fact, these might be my life messages...

Sean:

Nice. This conversation is really important. Let's keep at it.

Brad, I get that you're uncomfortable with God being "far away" and as an alternative to transcendence-as-distance you've suggested that "all the mysteries and transcendence of God are in Christ." What about "Our Father who art in heaven..." (Matthew 6:9)? Indeed, "Jesus is God, the fullness of the measure of God, who now knows all the mysteries of God, and expresses fully the character of God." And yet there's a mystery here too. Jesus also does not consider equality with God something to be grasped, but instead empties himself, taking on the form of a servant (Philippians 2). I'm a little uncomfortable here with what seems to be a one-sided Christocentric view of transcendence. Indeed, Jesus reveals God to us, but he also conceals God in certain ways too.

I like the Jenson quotation a lot. I just don't see how promises like "all that the Father has is mine" and "whatever the Spirit hears, he will make known to you" and "guide you into all truth" serve to "buckle the tension" between "now" and "not yet." If there's a buckling of the tension, in what sense does your affirmation of the "not yet" really apply in any practical sense? It seems like you are assuming that the promise somehow makes it a fact that we now enjoy a full knowledge of the truth under the guidance of the Spirit. I can see how a promise motivates hope and expectancy, but I'm not sure it should lead us to presume certain end results moment-by-moment if only we treat the promise seriously. So we trust that the Spirit reveals and guides and we listen and ask on this basis, but Jesus' promise does not serve to buckle the tension between hearing-obeying on the one hand and the waiting and wondering and expostulating and testing on the other.

Following your lead, I'm sensing a certain reactionary thinking on your part. I guess I'm not sure why you are having such a difficult time with the metaphor of distance in relation to divine transcendence. Jesus played on this trope all the time. The Father is in heaven, the Son on earth. The Son must go away to be with the Father, but he sends the Spirit. All the while, Father-Son-Spirit make up the Godhead.

Transcendence is about the holiness and sovereignty of the living God. God is far away and near at the same time. He invites us to come into his presence, but even in the face-to-face encounter there is as much distance between as nearness to (if we are to make capital on the spatial metaphor).

So there's an important sense in which God is unapproachable even at points of most intimate contact.

Brad:

There's a lot here. Let me start from the top.

I agree that we don't fully enjoy the promises that Jesus made concerning the Spirit. I just see them there. And then I understand that the gap between promise and enjoyment needs a response. Where God's promises and my life are not in alignment, I don't make a theology to excuse myself. I need to pursue the promise whole-heartedly and expectantly, without making demands on God or accusing him for breaking his promise.

I may be in reactionary mode, but unapproachable and intimate seems a contradiction rather than a paradox. The gospel does change our theology of transcendence. By the blood of Christ, we now approach the formerly unapproachable One boldly (Hebrews) and by the sanctification of the Spirit, we are transformed such that we are not consumed. This is all a work of grace through Christ who enables us to draw near and seats us in the heavenlies on the lap of a sovereign and holy God. This doesn't mean that I lose my dread or diminish God's awesome effects on certain of my encounters with him. But it leads me to think that transcendence is not *far-awayness*. It is a revelation we get by drawing close. Transcendence does not happen far away. It happens in encounter. Transcendence includes something mysterious and hidden, but this hiddenness is in the heart of the God I know, rather than simply the absence of God (though certainly it also includes times where he "feels" absent).

Concerning transcendence and the persons of the Trinity, I'd camp in John 14-16. The promise of the Spirit includes the promise that Father and Son will come and 1) make their home in us, and 2) show themselves to us. So with Pentecost, Jesus seems to be saying, "Yes, the Father is in heaven on his throne in his temple. And heaven's temple throne is in you and you are in it and on it with him." I know this is not the whole story, but this part of the story is completely true and real and to be experienced and enjoyed now. The "not yets" of it must co-exist with this. There is no "balance" to "we are seated with Christ in heavenly realms." It's just true and it's true all the time. Yet it's also true that my feet are on earth all the time. We have a habitation in heaven and on earth simultaneously, which works because via the Holy Spirit, heaven has been located (or in other texts, at least accessed) within.

I'm just not seeing God as so "far away" in the Scriptures after the arrival of Jesus... or certainly after Pentecost. If you're seeing it, point the way. What I hear is Paul in Athens, saying that he is not far from any of us because in him we live and move and have our being (Acts 17:27-28). I can't fathom a paradox that makes the ocean I'm immersed in far away, except if we just dial down the literalism of "far." Then it's easy: the height, width, and depth of his thoughts are "far" from within my grasp. And his love is "far" beyond my ability to comprehend. And his character, his sovereignty, his power, his holiness may be tasted and seen and experienced, but we barely know the first edge of it.

Sean:

Paradoxes can seem like contradictions, especially if we are privileging one side of the paradox over the other. I get the impression that you are treating God's imminence as foundational and primary given your reading of John 14-16, etc. and trying to make sense of transcendence in relation to it. And so it seems that you are coming close to assimilating transcendence to imminence. This is what I am hearing at least. I think your notion of transcendence is working in some ways, but it seems to create difficulties too.

This is a really important discussion, Brad. So much is happening for me as we dialogue together. And yet, while I find that I'm with you in some places, I feel distant in others. Again, I'm not sure what the role of a "not yet" has in the theology that you've outlined here. You've acknowledged it, but by the end it seems all but assimilated into the now.

Concerning God being far away after Pentecost, have a look at 1 Timothy 6:11-16:

> But you, man of God, flee from all this, and pursue righteousness, godliness, faith, love, endurance, and gentleness. Fight the good fight of the faith. Take hold of the eternal life to which you were called when you made your good confession in the presence of many

witnesses. In the sight of God, who gives life to every-thing, and of Christ Jesus, who while testifying before Pontius Pilate made the good confession, I charge you to keep this command without spot or blame until the appearing of our Lord Jesus Christ, which God will bring about in his own time—God, the blessed and only Ruler, the King of kings and Lord of lords, who alone is immortal and who lives in unapproachable light, whom no one has seen or can see. To him be honor and might forever. Amen.

Brad:

Nice. That's a bold and clear example of transcendence maintained after the incarnation and Pentecost (i.e. *after* Christ radicalized immanence). I'll rest on that.

" ͏

Here's the thing: I'm with you on the importance of uphold-ing the "not yet." It's just that John 16 does not seem to af-firm my theology of the "not yet" to the degree that I would assert or experience it. And I'm trying to practice the bowing of my theology and experience to Jesus' words. Yet I sense I'm not out to lunch and I know that John 16 is not the whole story. So the tension between the "now" and "not yet" buck-les, but doesn't break.

You ask if I'm "assuming that the promise makes it a fact that we now and forever enjoy a full knowledge of the truth under the guidance of the Spirit?"

First, no, we don't. But second, isn't that exactly what Jesus is saying? Words like "all" and "whatever" and "all" [again] are used purposefully. You, however, bring in the legitimate limits. He doesn't say "immediately" or "all at once." In fact, as a member of the Body of Christ, I don't think that I get the "all" myself (the church is supposed to) or that we will get it all "now" or even in my lifetime. Certain truths are just coming out that may make sense in 300 years... and the promise is still true.

My tensions aren't as much about imminence vs. transcendence as they are about putting my theology and experience through the fire of the red letters and finding that a fair bit is getting consumed.

It's true that "Jesus' promise does not serve to buckle the tension between hearing-obeying and waiting and wondering and expostulating and testing." With you.

Sean:

Of course, I would agree that Jesus' words are of paramount importance, but I'm wondering if "the practice of bowing [your] theology and experience to Jesus' words" is helpful in all cases. After all, Jesus is not claiming to say it all. Nor does he seem intent on filling out a totalizing picture. Should we be funneling all passages of Scripture through John 14-16 and other selected red letter passages? Hmm. What about the passages of Scripture that Jesus would heartily affirm even though they may seem to conflict with what he himself is quoted as saying in the gospels?

If it's true that "Jesus' promise does not serve to buckle the tension between hearing-obeying and waiting and wondering and expostulating and testing," what might this mean for Listening Prayer?

Brad:

It depends what you define as Listening Prayer. I define Listening Prayer as tuning in to the God who speaks. I define Listening Prayer as tuning into the many, many ways God speaks. I define Listening Prayer as tuning in *and* waiting and wondering and expostulating and testing what God speaks. In other words, you have just described Listening Prayer above rather well.

For those who collapse my entire teaching into moment-by-moment dialogue, I simply say something like this: "Have you read, forgotten or ignored chapter one in *Can You Hear Me?* "Listening Prayer" includes everything in the list at the end of chapter one and much, much more. If you are telling me that it 'doesn't work for you,' then I say, you aren't telling the truth. You mean to say that God never speaks to you through the Scriptures? You mean to say that God never convicts you of sin? You mean to say that God never gives you a burden to pray for others? You mean to say that God never prompts you to share or act in his name? And so on...

For the first two hours of every seminar, this is all I focus on: the many ways he is already speaking. I don't have to promise that they will hear. I show them how they do in fact hear.

On the other hand, if we were to reduce Listening Prayer to the inner healing conversations that I only bring in for the final chapter of the book (which would not be fair), this might sound odd, but I don't personally remember seeing the "not yet" of hearing apply in the last sixteen-plus years. That is, when it comes to the broken person who needs prayer for inner healing, I began to simply assume (not presume) that God would speak to them immediately after holding my breath for the first several years.

My experience was that this was just something he always does. But again, you can't predetermine the HOW. He might show himself, he might not. He might speak in sentence thoughts or in impressions that require articulation. He might require certain things to be done first, but even these he makes plain. He might encounter blocks, but he also shows us what they are and that he is the one who brought them up. In this very limited sense of Listening Prayer, his "heart" and his promise is to speak, and to those who are even blocked there, I assume it's precisely because they have a very limited sense of Listening Prayer.

Sean:

Interesting. Let me try to articulate something I'm seeing.

I'm not sure that the majority of your tentative readers/ listeners would disagree that God speaks in the more con-ventionally accepted ways that you spell out early on. I think some are coming away after reading the later parts of your book with the sense that God is speaking all the time, moment-by-moment, through Listening Prayer exercises/ encounters and that your argument in this respect seems to be in the service of subtlety overcoming the waiting and wondering and expostulating and testing. I realize that you do not actually claim such a thing in your book. It has more to do with your rhetorical style (it's actually a style that you practice in what you have just said above—hence the way that you come close to undoing what you say concerning the "not yet" of waiting and wondering by declaring a little further on that the "not yet" really hasn't applied in your experience as it relates to inner healing). And so, when such readers/listeners go through a dry spell or a time of disillusionment or disorientation, there doesn't seem to be the freedom to wait, wonder, rest, expostulate, test.

I've seen you help people to realize the ways in which they do in fact hear and this is really, really good. It can feel like a bit of a trick though when you go on to link up the regularity and conventionality of this kind of hearing with more direct, quasi-immediate Jesus encounters in Listening Prayer... again, I am only speaking to what it feels like (i.e. rhetorical strategy).

It seems a little odd to me that you haven't seen "the 'not yet' of hearing apply in so many years." Again, please keep in mind that I have no underlying agenda of creating a theology around a fully transcendent "not yet." You speak of leading the "broken person who needs prayer for inner healing" in Listening Prayer. "Broken" and "needs" are rather significant qualifiers, no? Not everyone is disposed like this from moment to moment. I wonder if the disposition of the people you've listened to/with doesn't have something to do with the relative immediacy of the answer.

I get the assumption (expectancy based on promise) of God speaking and I also understand the importance of inviting Jesus to speak now to these particular needs. Assuming that God will speak immediately seems different than this though. Hmm.

You acknowledge that we can't predetermine the "how." Is it really possible to predetermine anything?

Also, concerning your last point, is it really helpful to assume that someone is blocked if they are unable to hear God immediately?

Brad:

Last point first: Yes, I think so. It would puzzle me if someone came for this type of inner healing because of needs in their life and we were to ask God to throw us a bone and he said nothing at all. This would be like saying, "I have nothing at all to say to you today about your pain." That's not a Father.

You're right, we can't predetermine anything. But God can... and he has revealed some of his predeterminations to us. And it behooves us to believe him and trust him in these actively. When he says that he predetermines, "I will answer you,"

I would infer that it is wrong not to "call on him." When he predetermines to knock on the door of our hearts with a predetermination to enter and have an interactive supper, it is rude to hesitate to "open the door." When I proclaim this, I am vulnerable to the charge of presumption, but those who oppose what I've just said are also vulnerable to the charge of unbelief or even defiance against the predeterminations of Christ for those who say they follow him... whatever that means without some form of listening.

Here's where I'm coming from: God is speaking all the time, moment-by-moment, in that the flow of his heart and thoughts and voice never ceases. The outpouring never ceases. The radio station is always "on," perpetually messaging all of us with the love and glory and wonders of God through many channels (e.g. Psalm 19 says this explicitly).

Listening Prayer is a catch-all phrase for every way that we turn on and tune in our hearts. "Waiting" is another word for it—a very biblical word for it. Those who "wait" on the Lord are practicing Listening Prayer. Those who wait on the Lord are taught and promised in Scripture to expect to receive something, to find something, to hear something. So first comes the waiting. Then... there is really not much else to do until we DO hear or receive something. In other words, you can't weigh and test a nothing. A something will come as you wait (God says so). Only when there is a something to test do we begin that process.

Where I feel you resisting is when I suggest that the waiting is generally not as long as we make it out to be. (i.e. you're resisting an expectation of a moment-by-moment conversation... which, by the way, I regard as different from an immediate answer to my agenda questions).

The reason I am optimistic about the moment-by-moment stuff is based on some simple Jesus math:

- He's my best friend, wonderful counselor, shepherd king.
- I'm his beloved child.
- He's with me all the time, bathing me with his presence.
- He never leaves. He is always before me. He is at my right hand all the time.
- He says he'll answer when I call and that "speedily."

(I know he doesn't mean this absolutely, but he seems to imply that I should expect it. When he doesn't answer speedily, that raises new questions... and I find that he answers them).

Example: a camp director calls and asks if I can speak on a certain date and says, I'll let you pray about it. So I say, okay ... hang on a minute. [pause: where is Jesus at that moment? Does he care if I speak at that retreat? What does "pray about it" mean? Ask him? If I ask my Lord (as in my boss), who is at my right hand all the time (Acts 2), should I speak at that retreat, why would he take two weeks to answer me? Or one week? Why not just ask and see what he says? Does he need to think about it?] And in about thirty seconds, I tell the guy, "Yeah, I can come." He's beside himself. Why?

Well, here's what's going on. I'm treating Jesus as a real person who is actually with me. Someone who has called me his friend and who also requires me to enquire. Period. That's all. And that's really, really offensive OR really, really surprising when you actually practice it. In fact, it looks stupid. It looks like you've got an imaginary friend. I don't. I just have an invisible friend. Not a slot machine, but true God and true man, living with and in and through me. And so do you.

So then testing and weighing is about making sure that your invisible friend is not a figment of your imagination, a projection of your ego or a demon.

I get what you're saying about my rhetorical approach. It's just what has happened, that's all. I oversimplify when I say that I expect based on promises. What I mean is this: I started seeing the promises in Scripture. I didn't expect them, but I tried them. After holding my breath for years (because I still didn't believe that these were promises), I experienced that he was faithful to his promise every time until I stopped holding my breath. So now I just assume that he's made his point, based on experience-tested biblical promises.

If I am in a dry spell or feeling disillusioned and disoriented, what I do and counsel others to do, if there are indeed no blocks in their life, is to go back to the practices in chapter one. Dry? How about picking up the Psalms, turning on a CD, and sitting with a cup of coffee. How about asking something as basic as "do you love me?" How about going for a walk outside and letting nature bless you with God's goodness.

See what I'm doing? I'm just trying a few different exercises. Maybe this is the "aha" for me today: that *"waiting" is a Listening Prayer exercise and Listening Prayer is just another term for "waiting"...* not idleness.

Dwight:

Brad, if waiting, as you've described it here is part of listening, then I've been doing Listening Prayer for years.

I think sometimes I allowed the idea of Listening Prayer to short circuit waiting, when I had already developed trust for a certain way of hearing. However, I began to wonder if maybe I was to hear differently. And I think I have learned to broaden the set of wavelengths I'm tuned to. But I'm also getting more comfortable with "silence" again.

Brad:

I am also comfortable sitting in silence with the Lord. At the same time, I caution people to beware of returning to the comfort of practical deism.

I think that the call to expectancy can also trigger a pressure in us for a need to come up with something. We don't need to come up with something. But we do need to listen, even to the silence.

Dwight:

Yes. I'm good with that. I believe God speaks immediately, over time, and in various ways. I do not doubt that at all. I don't think I ever have.

What your thoughtful teaching and experience has done is to help me notice different places and ways in which God is speaking, a point you have noted. It has also given me confidence that I have been hearing from God for years.

Brad, I want to affirm as well that you have encouraged me to trust God more in the immediate. Although I always believed he would answer, I used to do a lot of weighing/ discerning over things, gathering as much information as possible, and sorting it out. I was always prayerful about it mind you, and sometimes God seemed to answer immediately, too. I think I was also fearful of missing the point he was making, but I'd need to reflect a little more to ascertain whether it was dread, as discussed elsewhere, or slavish fear. I'd like to believe it was more of the former.

I think it helps that I grew up with a mother who taught me to pray about specific things, in the moment, and we have stories to tell that have kept me going even on this journey.

Brad:

I have some thoughts about your experience in particular and waiting in silence in general.

In your case, would it be true that the waiting in silence part is largely about accessing peace in times of decision or burden when the Lord has not yet given direction? That is, you wait in silence, rather than needing to wrack your brains about the next move, while at the same time, God continues to speak to you through his Word, through the Body, continuing to convict of sin and righteousness, continuing to express his love, call you to intercede, and so on.

In other words, that "God is silent" is true, but it's also an overstatement that should be qualified with "... about my next step." But he is certainly not utterly silent. God seems very, very silent when I over-privilege directional content as the only thing he would possibly say to me. I don't sense you're saying that. You sound like you've just found that waiting is okay when God is not pulling the trigger yet on your next move.

In this regard, I wonder if some of the old angst was about weighing and testing before he's spoken... which feels like trying to ring water out of a rock.

Dwight:

Spot on. It can be a weird space, though. I don't usually mind it personally, but I often get the impression that other people think it's irresponsible or unwise. And because I believe in the discernment of the Body, I begin to ask, "God, are you telling them something you're not telling me?! Please don't!" So, then, I've gone around probing for more information when I could be content to just wait for the voice of God to be heard at the right time.

Brad:

I know what you mean.

Now back to our concerns for those who really do have trouble hearing... I want them to hear this: "YOU are okay. Not hearing is not okay insofar as we're commanded to hear. So if something's broken, let's look at it. Here's a book that might help." I didn't write the book for those who hear easily, but for those who have never tried, never realized they could or who have a really rough time with it. If one of my suggestions doesn't help every single person who wants to hear God better, then it's not the perfect and final work to be written on the subject. But I gave it a shot.

Admittedly, I didn't see fit to write a chapter on why it's okay not to hear God's voice. I thought that we have enough of those around stealing otherwise good seed.

I'm counseling that we continue the regular practices in an intentional, quasi-immediate way. That is, instead of praying for just anyone, I ask which loved one I might pray for. Instead of composing my own list of sins to confess, I ask the Holy Spirit to convict me of what offends him. Instead of memorizing and listing the promises of God, I ask him to remind me of a promise. All of these are conventional, but by putting these conventional prayers back in God's hands, I'm building myself up in the faith that he will have other things on his heart to share.

In other words, I'm not adding Listening Prayer as additional items to a list which begins with conventional items. I'm saying that the conventional items can be done easily, by any three-year-old, in a listening kind of way which transforms a recital into a conversation. Then, when you find out that he'll speak to you about your regular adoration, confession, thanksgiving, supplication things, just keep talking. Is there anything else on your heart to bring to him? The biggest barrier to overcome is our unbelief that "what comes to mind" might be God. So in every seminar or one-on-one and also in the book, I ask, "Okay, don't say, 'God told me.' Just tell me what came to mind." NOW let's weigh that and consider whether that might be him.

Sean, you say it's odd that the "not yet" did not come to bear in my experience with healing. It seemed a little odd to me too—at least for the first year or two. Now it seems more like, "Well, if God loves them and is committed to comforting them and bearing ALL their sorrows as he says in Isaiah 53, I guess it's not so odd." People don't usually think I'm a skeptic by nature... I am. I'm just a skeptic whose been convinced the hard way.

Yeah, "broken" and "needs" are significant qualifiers. A few things here: Who isn't broken? Who has no needs? Are they too small for him? If your need is as big as a sparrow, then his heart is towards you already. But also, it is very true that the greatly needy seem to hear most clearly and dramatically, which jives well with the Scriptures that talk about God being close (in a special way) to the brokenhearted and crushed in spirit. The strange result is that it's easier for someone who has been raped to hear God in a clear and powerful way than someone who is simply offended by a brother. I could probably speculate about why this is, but I also don't want to overstate it... because drama isn't a valid test.

You say "assuming that God will speak immediately seems different." Maybe only by degrees. The way it's worked has been this: It moves from extreme to normal. I would see God visit a painful memory and ask, what about any memory, even good ones? I would see God completely lift off the trauma of gang-rape and ask, what about any burden, even simple guilt? I would see God create a safe place for people who did, and ask, what about the rest of us (if Psalm 23 is true)? And every time, what I would hear was, "I thought you'd never ask." And so I'd try it (again, holding my breath for the first twenty times) and find out that his responsiveness is not restricted to the specially or profoundly broken, but to all who call on his name.

This has been another "aha" moment for me: *God is the most responsive person in the universe, and this is because it is predicated on his initiative.*

Sean:

I appreciate so much of what you've said here... Dwight too... especially concerning the relationship between waiting, listening, and trusting. I still find myself resisting in parts though...

It seems to me that there are different kinds of divine speech in Scripture. Yes, there's a kind of divine speech pouring forth from day to day (Psalm 19), but I'm not sure that we should be equating that kind of speech with a more direct form that says, "Son of man, stand on your feet that I may speak with you!" (Ezekiel 2:1). It would be very peculiar to suggest that God is always broadcasting in this way. Again, this does not mean that we shouldn't be tuning in, listening, asking, calling out. However, I'm not sure that we should be expecting there's a message akin to the latter if only we put up our antennae. (?)

Concerning your understanding of brokenness in relation to Listening Prayer, of course we are all broken in a sense and in need of God's goodness, but from moment to moment we are not all requiring critical attention. I'm thinking that it's significant that a person comes to you and expresses particular needs, requesting prayer. This is different than a person who doesn't recognize herself as broken or in a critical situation of need.

Thinking about your final point about hearing God immediately through inner-healing conversations...

I can imagine not getting a specific, directed response about someone's pain in the moment. I don't see how this would conflict with the goodness of God. Again, the potentiality of not receiving such a response is not a pretext for refusing to ask. No, no. We ask and we listen and we rejoice when we are answered (and we trust that we will in fact be answered). And this becomes confidence for more asking and listening.

Brad:

Helpful. I think I've overstated something a wee bit. The broken do hear very well as a gift of grace during something like trauma counseling when we go there. And the worse the pain, the more powerfully God seems to come (this is a generalization).

But then I started asking myself, what other groups generally hear ESPECIALLY well and a few came to mind... those we regard as "the pillars" of Fresh Wind:

- prodigals coming home
- children
- people with disabilities
- the poor

And there were others, but I started to look for common points among the groups. Childlike trust covered a couple of the groups. Humility seemed to cover all of them. Biblically, another word for this might be fear of the Lord. Some scriptures came to mind:

- James 4:6 – "God opposes the proud, but gives grace to the humble."
- Psalm 138:6 – "[God] cares for the lowly and knows the proud from afar."
- Psalm 25:14 – "The Lord confides in those who fear him."

So while his Spirit may be poured out on all flesh, God also privileges some to a closer experience:

> • Isaiah 66:2 – "And to such shall I look—to the poor, to the broken in spirit and to those who tremble at my word."
> • Isaiah 57:15 – "I live with... him who is contrite and lowly in spirit."

And out of this, I thought, I don't need to become one of the pillars (become a recovering addict or regress to being five-years-old or develop a disability or go bankrupt), but I could purpose to become pillar-like: learn the fear of the Lord, invest in humility, develop a lowly and contrite heart... which of course reminded me that I'd written on this (posture of a listener) already.

Anyway, I just wanted to say that while we've talked about a unique kind of listening that I see in working with the broken, they are not the only group that hears exceptionally, and it's not their brokenness that tunes up their ears, but a shift in their hearts that amplifies God's voice. This shift is something that we can all foster, even those who are fairly healthy and relatively wealthy, who are more intelligent than simple, more analytical than visceral, and more prone to pride than humility. It just requires some discipline in areas where the pillars get there through their natural circumstance.

It is our pillars who train us in this.

Sean:

Yes, this is really important as it relates to your presentation of Listening Prayer and I think it's generally true.

There's also this: those who have been hurt often carry with them a ferocious need for justice, especially in cases where the hurt has taken place in the dark and the abusers cannot see the relevance of the wrong and/or refuse to acknowledge culpability. Of course, this need for justice is entirely understandable and it arises within us precisely because of our status as bearers of God's image (Genesis 1:26).

However, it can also leave us in a kind of dilemma when it consumes our hearts and minds. That is, it is possible for those of us who have experienced significant hurt at the hands of others to cope and even become open to God's goodness and grace, but it's really difficult for us to feel right about ourselves or God until justice has finally been done to those who have hurt us. In the meantime, we hold onto our pain because it's the only means of verifying that a past injustice has in fact been done and it seems like the only ticket to seeing justice finally exacted against our abusers.

As my inclusive language suggests, this is not a unique story. We have all lived through it in various ways—some with brutal and inconceivable intensity, others less so. The point is this: there's a way in which the hurt that we have received at the hands of others can lend itself not only to vulnerability before God and an openness to divine grace and freedom, but also to a form of self-justification that refuses full relationship prior to retribution.

Here's the thing: that we would allow God to bear what we cannot can seem grossly intolerable when we're conscious of having suffered injustice and this because it seems to require that we give up the only thing that will finally ensure that we get the justice we deserve.

It seems to me that there's a subtle accusation of God in all this that prevents healing and wholeness and lends itself to various distortions concerning ourselves and God...

One thing we'll likely miss is the way that the injustice we've suffered and the desire for reparations comes home in the self-giving love of Jesus.

Brad:

When someone has a genuine meeting at the cross, the fruit I've seen is that pain and hurt and anger can be released and (not sure if "because") justice is satisfied in their hearts. It is absolutely essential that God does not simply negate any of that, but that he bears it all in his arms and hands (i.e. the pain, the anger, the hurt, and the offender). The person seems to get a revelation that the offender is not off the hook. Merely off THEIR hook and in God's merciful AND just hands. There is such a thorough sense of PENDING justice that there is trust and contentment and relief... sort of like the period when a criminal offender is already in custody and perhaps already convicted. Just a matter of trusting a perfect judge with the right sentence... which is why they can often pray for mercy for their offender.

Sean:

It's so difficult to believe that God can bear it in the way that is best. It's so easy to overlook Jesus in our need for justice. I'm with you on what a genuine meeting at the cross looks like.

I was trying to articulate some of the barriers that we have in meeting Jesus at the cross. One of the main ones is our need for justice. The nature of the Accuser's lie in Genesis 3 implies it. "You'll get what you rightly deserve from God" is the subtext...

Brad:

For sure... A while back you expressed concern about a lack of practical relevance of the "not yet" in my understanding of Listening Prayer. Three "not yets" that seem particularly relevant:

    1. "Not yet" because Christ has not returned for the final consummation. Some promises are simple not "already." They await "that day."

    2. "Not yet" because some of the "already" promises await the proper time and place in God's unfolding plan.

3. "Not yet" because some of the "already" promises require a capacity of faith/belief that can receive them.

Number three troubles me because whenever I see it in the gospels, Jesus rebukes his disciples. But when I see it in the church, we borrow "not yet" theology to justify our immaturity and lack of authority. This troubled me less when no one around me was getting healed (maybe it's not for now) than it does when I see five to twenty percent of those we pray for get healed (we suck at this).

I'm also troubled when those who see the twenty percent getting healed are accused of presumption (Note: I haven't heard accusations here. Just valid questions and loving warnings) as if God were annoyed when they assume more should be getting healed. When they accuse God, yes, it's presumption. When they confess, help us believe, it's not presumption. We see that Jesus is powerful, had called us to operate in his authority, and that our sporadic success highlights a deficiency in us (not in God or in the unhealed).

And I'm troubled when "not yet" is used as a disclaimer in the same way we used "thy will be done." Why? Because in that case, "not yet" is being used to plug our ears from any rebuke that might be forthcoming.

And finally, I'm troubled when the triumphalists and the presumptuous and the theologically sloppy heal MANY more of the sick than we do. It's not fair. Specifically, I know of a Vineyard style church that finally renounced the "not yet" intentionally and started preaching that "of course it's God's heart that all would be healed. Just look at Jesus." The shift was dramatic. Major healings started breaking out. I won't go into some of the stories, but they are beyond what I've seen firsthand. If the theological shift isn't the active ingredient, something is... maybe the expectancy. I don't know. These aren't the charlatans or hucksters. They aren't doing the faith-healer circuit. It's just a community that found "not yet" (version three) had to be acknowledged and removed. And it worked. And that troubles me.

Sean:

This is really helpful. I'm tracking with you here.

It's interesting that all three versions of the "not yet" can be abused. So you find it troubling that we would make number three a permanent condition in order "to justify our immaturity and lack of authority." Me too. This is partly my story and I've seen how it has diminished the abundant life that Jesus promised.

To add to this, I find it troubling that we would attempt to overcome the "not yet" of numbers one and two by charting grand eschatological schemes in a quasi-scientific way (from Lindsell to LaHaye and Jenkins) and then propagating them as the "absolute truth," thereby justifying a similar "immaturity," but with different results. The abuse of number three leads to a complacent deferral of what has already been revealed and what we have in fact been called

61

to participate in. The abuse of numbers one and two leads to a presumptuous enforcement of what we can only guess at for now and what we have not been invited to participate in at all. Both abuses are motivated by an inordinate fear and show a preference for a god that is dead rather than alive. If we would learn to trust the living God at his Word and love him with all our hearts-minds-souls, we would listen rather than presume, ask rather than possess and impose.

And in the listening and asking, we would discover ourselves as those who've been called to participate in the coming of God's kingdom—a kingdom defined by self-giving love rather than fear, hypocrisy, and manipulation. Enough of the "gospel of bondage" that would zap the legitimate confidence that is ours in Christ while allowing the overconfidence that wells up from a deceitful heart to win the day.

You've probably been wondering where I'm coming from in this conversation because I haven't really affirmed much of what you've said along the way. Important things are happening for me at this end though. You need to understand that I am not resisting you or the fruit of listening/obedience in your life. What I've been reacting to is some of your theological presentation. My sense is that the resistance has been important because I think you've been led to emphasize some things over others in reaction to certain camps of naysayers. As I've listened you seem to feel that a theology that upholds a more traditional view of transcendence would somehow do an injustice to what you've witnessed concerning people getting healed. I'm suggesting that it does nothing of the sort. In fact, it only helps to clarify what's happening.

It seems to me that your view of transcendence/imminence is unduly affected by the way that they are abused by cessationists and charismatics alike rather than the way that they are presented across the Scriptures as a whole.

Brad:

Yes, exactly! And this awareness came for me first as confession (as in the Introduction to *Can You Hear Me?*): "We err because we do not know the Scriptures or the power of God" (Matthew 22:29) and "We have a form of godliness but deny the power thereof" (2 Timothy 3:5). And we're really, really good at it! So my journey began with those confessions.

Why are we virtually unrecognizable from the church of Acts? "Silver and gold have I none. But such as I have give I thee. In the name of Jesus Christ of Nazareth, rise up and walk" (Acts 3:6). That haunts me. What did he have? "Authority over every kind of sickness and disease and over all the power of the enemy" (Matthew 10:1). Either we don't have that because we have not waited for power from on high or we do have it and don't know how to wield it.

Sean:

Nice. I'm seeing things in a very different light at this point.

Again, my sense is that certain aspects of your theology around Listening Prayer are unduly influenced by a desire on your part to provide the confidence we need to entrust ourselves fully to God and his purposes. It seems to me that this desire creates the conditions for overstatement and so you end up coming close at times to collapsing the theological paradoxes that are necessary to affirm and even heighten.

Here's the thing: you need not even begin to try and figure out how it all shakes down theologically at the outset. Nor should you be unduly concerned about the various ways in which certain theological notions are and have been abused. We need to hear you speak to the promises from Scripture, we need to hear you try to take them seriously, and we desperately need to hear you bear witness to the way in which the Spirit is moving. There's no need to drive to theological conclusions though, saying, in effect, "here's how you can count on God working according to the theology I've laid out." The confidence to trust God fully comes from somewhere other than theological demonstration.

Brad:

This really helps. I am certainly trying to make a case for the voice of God and suggesting ways we might tune into that voice. Can you expand a little on what you think I should be doing instead?

Sean:

I believe that you do not need to make a case for anything. When you set about building a case you are actually working against the nature of the thing that you would give voice to. You are playing the role of lawyer rather than witness.

Playing the role of lawyer presumes that the truth of your presentation is subject to the judgment of an earthly judge/jury. However, since you are trying to give voice to the fruit of listening/obedience, you are primarily a witness.

Let your theology be predictable. Spoon it out like pabulum. Spend the vast majority of your time testifying to the promises and bearing witness to the fruit. That's the real meat.

I think this is why Paul says so confidently,

> I care very little if I am judged by you or by any human court; indeed, I do not even judge myself. My conscience is clear, but that does not make me innocent. It is the Lord who judges me. Therefore judge nothing before the appointed time; wait till the Lord comes. He will bring to light what is hidden in darkness and will expose the motives of men's hearts. At that time each will receive his praise from God. (1 Corinthians. 4:3-5)

Don't feel obligated or compelled to respond to your critics in polemical ways. Just keep bearing witness to the good things that the Lord is doing as you seek to trust and obey. Also, continue looking to your visioning team for guidance.

Brad:

Good. I've learned to love submission and authority in the church. They are not a threat any more. They are a fortress.

Sean:

If there is a calling to respond, it will be most helpful for you to assume and play to a generally orthodox theology and interpretive practice, even as you seek to bear witness to the (unexpected) fruit of listening/obedience.

Brad:

Good. I work on this at seminars, trying even to gear to specifically Baptist or Anglican or United or Pentecostal language when possible. To some, I come with "the prophetic," to others, "the contemplative," to others, the "Word says," and that usually helps. That's why most of my detractors are not normally rising out of congregations where I've been in person.

Sean:

Mmmhmm. Assume that you and your cautious reader want the same thing, but avoid putting words/thoughts in mouths/minds of your interlocutors. Try to anticipate where you will likely miss each other, but guard against presumption.

Try to sympathize with the perspective of the "other" even as you attend to the reality that you've come to know. Double vision is key.

Avoid looking for common ground theologically.

Brad:

Why wouldn't I? Tell me about this.

Sean:

In love, let the other be other. If there are connections to be made, let the other make them. Again, you are not trying to convince or persuade. You are bearing witness.

When you get hung up, come back to the stories.

Brad:

That's handy. I've instinctively done this, at times even during this conversation. It's good to know that it's "allowed."

I remember going there with one of your staff once. We were hashing through John 10 and really seeing it differently, so I just shared a testimony. He really listened carefully and then commented the next day that he hadn't slept much the night after our conversation. When I asked why that was, he said, "It was the story."

Sean:

So, bear witness *more* rather than less.

Brad:

Good. Will do.

I think part of the disconnect is that I'm not intending to say, "here's how you can count on God working according to the theology I've laid out." It's more like: "Scripture pointed me in a certain direction. Pastoral experience confirmed it. And the mystical theologians confirmed it. All three bring me to the same conclusion: The church can count on hearing a God who speaks if they will but listen. This is what God wants the church to know and practice. My job is to testify to that."

Perhaps when I am testifying to how I see a biblical assertion put into practice, a theologian will assume I'm laying out a theology. Or when a theologian challenges me theologically and I answer as best I can, it sounds like I'm laying out a theology. I'm not sure I lay out theologies unless pressed to do so. Certainly at the seminars, I perceive myself to be putting some scriptures and stories on the table and then saying, "if these were true... well, let's see if they're true..." and we do some exercises.

Indeed "the confidence to trust God fully comes from somewhere other than theological demonstration." I'm trying to think like Alvin Plantinga. After accumulating sufficient warrant to "know" that God speaks, I want to reproduce this by gathering sufficient warrant to bring others to that same knowledge (i.e. 1. Scriptural warrant, 2. The testimony of the church over the centuries, 3. The testimony of my own witness through stories, 4. The warrant of personal experience through the exercises). I don't see it as a theological demonstration. I watch confidence grow as warrant is assembled. Dealing with blocks addresses the issues of proper function. Warrant is insufficient for knowledge when one's environment (e.g. the belief system of their home, church or school) is broken or when one's own apparatus for assessing warrant (e.g. personal unbelief, various blocks, broken heart) is damaged.

Now, I've just responded philosophically, but my confidence isn't based in laying out a philosophy either. Both theology and philosophy are fancy ways we talk about why I asked the pregnant lady at the coffee shop yesterday where Jesus would be during her delivery. Or why her two year old dragged her over to me to confess to a stranger that she has OCD (obsessive-compulsive disorder) during pregnancy. Or how, when she found out how I was, she already knew that God would send her to me... how could I possibly presume God would answer such questions in a coffee shop while we're standing there? I don't think about that then. I just do it, just as perhaps Peter just did it (times 1000) in Acts 3. But why I do it has this back-story which can be described in limited ways (more than prescribed) theologically or philosophically. Yet I didn't arrive there through those means. In fact, just the opposite. The theology is derived inductively through years of pregnant women with pointing two-year-olds in coffee shops. And while that might not be proper theology, it's akin to Peter's processing in Acts 3. (with the same results... called to give account by theologians who wanted to know by what authority they did and said such things)... except I have an extra burden... to equip a generation of churches who respond to pregnant OCD sufferers in the moment because that's how life works normally on the front lines.

Sean:

Good, good. Here's my advice: Let the back-story come to the front.

I say this for a couple of reasons: 1) I have been most personally impacted by your testimony of the Spirit's work; 2) your many experiences with listening/obedience are not in fact the back story even though you tend to play them as such. They are not mere examples of some more primary abstracted truth. Again, you are bearing witness to the good fruit that you've come to know rather than making a case for doctrinal truths that we've never really known. I've heard some scholarly readers refer to the problem of the book's thesis. I can understand why they speak this way, but you don't really need to argue a point as a prelude to the kind of work that you're doing. I love that you draw on Scripture widely, but why would you quote from the Scriptures as though you are building a case for an undiscovered reality? Rather than using them to defend a position or convince those who lack awareness or confidence, let them continue to give shape to your practice of listening and obedience and let them continue to breathe life into what you've encountered. The beautiful part is that you don't need to say how it all hangs together. You're allowed to admit to uncertainty (like you've done here many times). Sometimes it'll be relevant to attempt a connection or two, but again, make the connections by drawing on long established theologies and well-worn passages of Scripture. Again, your testimony is the meat, the theological explanation the pabulum.

David:

Hold on. Shouldn't testimony enter into conversation with Scripture finally, if it is to be grounded? I'm thinking of Paul here...

Sean:

Yes. And I'm suggesting that it needs to. But in Brad's case, he need not allow a scholarly approach to the Scriptures to take precedence. That is, he need not fill out a theology of Listening Prayer through a detailed biblical exegesis in order to make space for the fruit of listening/obedience that is in fact occurring. The promises of Scripture are really important and they don't require much exegetical analysis in order to be recognized as such. I'm thinking that we fail to notice God's promises and treat them seriously not because they are difficult to recognize, but because we fail to read the Scriptures in light of the living Word.

It's a common theme in Scripture and Nietzsche bore testimony to it in relation to the church of his own day: We'd rather live as though God were dead rather than alive. It's significant that Brad is drawing our attention to God's promises and trying to treat them seriously.

David:

Hmm... I expect I'm restating what you've already talked about: I agree that Brad doesn't need to let a polemical or a legal-argumentative approach take precedence; he doesn't have to say "case closed." But irenic theology-as-conversation is a necessary part of testimony, it seems to me.

Consider the Mormons: I don't accept everyone's testimony—it needs to fit into the authoritative story-line to which I am committed. Even then, I don't know what to do with some people's testimony because they are so far outside the realm of my experience. In these cases, Scripture speaks louder.

Sean:

Yes, hear you. I'm assuming, though, that Brad would be identifying himself as a Christian and a pastor and be expressing a commitment to following the Scriptures closely (without filling in all the complexities of what this means) and working in concert with the community of faith. So a recognition of fiduciary-biblical-ecclesial bounds is crucial.

I'm simply saying that, within these bounds, Brad should spend most of his time focusing on the fruit of listening/obedience rather than clearing the ground for Listening Prayer. He needs to draw attention to what's happening by bearing witness rather than proving what should happen by making a case.

David:

And by "bearing witness" you include saying: "Here's my

experience, and here's how I see it lining up with scripture"?

Sean:

Sure. But what do you mean by "lining up"? I'm not trying to play games here. The logician understands "lining up" very differently than those of a more poetic sensibility (poetic in the most biblical sense of the term).

David:

Lining up. Scripture testifies to my testimony.

Sean:

Yeah, that's good. At the same time though, Scripture itself does not have agency and so Brad will always be vulnerable to the charge of making Scripture say what he wants it to when attempting to line things up after the fact.

I think it's really important for him to indicate a different sort of lining up with Scripture—one that actually comes prior to experience—that is, his effort to treat the promises of Jesus seriously.

It would also be really helpful for him to provide a rudimentary testing/weighing in the course of bearing witness by calling to mind biblical passages in a suggestive rather than quasi-scholarly manner. This would constitute a kind of lining up, but not one of one-for-one correspondence. Whatever the case, I think for now, at least in the public eye, he should avoid the extra step of reflecting theologically and making seeming-definitive claims about how God does and doesn't work given what he's experienced.

His approach should be funded by Scripture, but we should not expect him to establish warrant for a theology of Listening Prayer and nor should he. Given that he is a witness rather than a lawyer/defendant, Brad should be assuming a different kind of warrant, a kind of warrant that he already has within ecclesial bounds. That is, Brad is a member of the body of Christ and, as such, he has all the warrant he needs to bear witness to the good things that God is doing through listening/obedience within his community of faith. We need to weigh the testimony, but the weighing would have an entirely different quality under these conditions.

Also, it's really important to notice that Brad is not bearing witness to a new revelation from God. Some have thought that this is what he's doing, and it can come across this way, especially in places where he's building a case for something new called "Listening Prayer," but this is not what he's up to. His main concern is to do justice to the fruit of listening/obedience that he has experienced under the authority of the Scriptures and in consultation with his visioning team at Fresh Wind.

I think it's entirely possible for Brad to do what he's doing and remain centered in "mere Christianity."

I'm saying that he needs to spend more time telling us about what he's doing and allowing the Scriptures to provide direction, confidence, and correction, but he need not speak to all the whys and wherefores (even though he may have some very good ideas about them).

When pressed to draw conclusions about how God works in a grand theological sense, he's allowed to confess ignorance or to speak in very elementary terms according to a broadly accepted theology or well worn passages of Scripture. If the theologians and exegetes have a problem with this, let them do their best to remedy it.

Glenn:

Whatever Brad is doing, it is the theologians among us who are responsible to fill in some of the gaps, make some of the connections.

I don't think we can forget here, that Brad is a theologian... and a good one. The work that he has been called to do could only be done by a theologian, but the work that he is doing is not theology.

Brad:

Nice. I know and intended to be a witness, not a lawyer. I don't mind letting people come to their own conclusions. I need to be much more mindful about the tendency to slip back.

I think that I tend to move towards lawyer when someone makes a case against the teaching. It's hard to resist going to the theological dock when I enjoy theology and that was my area of training (I took every theology and Bible course that Briercrest offered at the time, including the correspondence courses... I loved it). I also wonder if I insert my conclusions when I'm preparing to go from scripture/testimony into the exercises. Can you suggest an appropriate segue?

Sean:

What do you mean?

Brad:

Well, Scripture testifies to a speaking God.
My testimony testifies to a speaking God.
Therefore, I conclude that God speaks. Let's give it a try...
Should I be skipping the third line?
If I do, should I replace it with something else?

Sean:

Yes, skip the "therefore." It's not needed. After all, you are not trying to set up a syllogism. Should you replace it with something? Hmm. Perhaps a rhetorical question instead of a logical conclusion? Something like: "what's preventing us from listening in together right now?"

Again, bearing witness is the really important thing.

After telling a story about corporate Listening Prayer at The Gathering, a person strongly opposed to Listening Prayer said to me, "Well yeah, that's really important. It seems like you were caught up together in the Spirit" as though that were somehow categorically different than what can happen in Listening Prayer.

Brad:

Can you say a little more about the story?

Sean:

At Sunday Gathering, Kevin F. focused us on Acts 12, specifically the episode in which Peter is miraculously released from prison while his "house church" is praying for him. We had kids/adults act it out. One thing in particular stood out: the people were praying fervently and yet they were astonished when their prayers had been answered. This was significant in its own right, but it provided a bit of a prelude for discussing a matter of urgency for our church community. A member who had long suffered from debilitating depression had attempted to end her life and was now in the hospital in critical condition. She too was in a dark place, a prison of sorts, and we needed to plead with the Lord for her release. Will we be astonished? Hmm.

Kevin invited us to prepare our hearts through a time of worship and thanksgiving. As we were singing, I was already in full dialogue with the Lord and he gave me a word, so in the middle of the set I shared from the front. I spoke to the fascination of the Herod figure in the story and how easy it is to get distracted by him and play to his "power," imagining a covert operation of sorts to spring our loved one from prison. I said that we needed to entrust ourselves to the almighty God rather than compete with Herod. There was a kind of confirmation in the moment because I noticed a number of nodding heads, but one person in particular came to Kevin after I sat down and related a word that she had received and when she shared, it partly confirmed the word that I had shared and unfolded things a bit further. We then prayed together and it was rather electric. One man broke down in tears, crying out for God to intervene like any good father would for one of his children in distress. This was un- settling to say the least, but we wept with him and asked the living God to loose the chains and set the captive free. AND HE DID (more on that another time). Interestingly, a little girl played the part of Peter when we acted out the story at the beginning of the service. This was because none of the boys wanted to. Some people recognized this as a providen- tial sign when reflecting on the service afterwards...

I related this to the person so strongly opposed to Listening Prayer. I was intrigued by the effect of bearing witness rather than discussing theologically. We hadn't made much progress in our discussion concerning Listening Prayer, but when I wit- nessed to a specific instance of Listening Prayer in a corporate church setting, he was able to hear me in a way. Interestingly, he was entirely comfortable with the kind of listening and hearing that we had been engaged in. "We need more of this rather than less," he said. He was also comfortable with the allegorical "application" of the text because there were no claims being made concerning the "authoritative meaning."

He was concerned to know two things about my experience in hearing from the Lord: 1) Did I "go to a *meeting place*"—as per in chapter five of *Can You Hear Me?*—a bad thing in his mind; and 2) Was I visualizing (i.e. projecting—again, a bad thing).

I told him that I did not personally identify the listening encounter with God in terms of a *meeting place*, but I saw no reason not to on reflection. There was a middle ground for listening and seeing and it would make entire sense to call it a *meeting place* since I met the Lord there (or rather he met me). I also said that there was much visualization going on in the listening. After all, I was stepping into the story so it was impossible not to. But I was not merely engaged in an "exercise" (another concern for him). Things would occur to me as I watched the story unfold in my heart's eye. I would ask the Lord about them and more would occur to me. And then I would look again and see other things. And so on. He just sat silently listening. I also told him that my confidence in listening/obeying in this way was significantly influenced by your work on Listening Prayer.

Brad:

Thanks for this. Sometimes when we write back and forth, I can see my movement but have a hard time discerning yours.

I was going to ask you about that. How or where have you moved in all this?

Sean:

You mean in this conversation specifically? I'm not sure that I've moved as in changed my mind about key issues. I can tell you that my confidence has only grown concerning the object of your "life messages"—that is, 1) heeding the Jesus of the Gospels, and 2) meeting Jesus in the now.

In this sense, I've moved much. Again, what gets me most is the way that you simply press through and practice what you preach. There's no deferral. You listen and obey. This is what's challenging me the most. Yes, it's moving me significantly.

Brad:

Thanks. Sometimes it's hard to see the fruit in you during the resisting stages. But then when you reflect and say, "here's how I've grown," I realize that this is not all about cornering me until I change my mind and you are finally proven right. I don't see it that way, but I think where and why you are moving in the discussion occasionally needs to be articulated.

Sean:

I hear you. I can argue a point pretty hard if I'm convinced. I can tell you that in this context, I argue hard because there's something coming to me in the space between us. It's weird, but I'm trying to bear witness to an emergent truth rather than prove a point. I'm trying to keep troth—with you, with Jesus, with the Agora community.

Glenn used this analogy some time ago. He imagined you as a deep-sea diver and me as the one giving out the line as you go down into the depths. Glenn thought it was really important for you to have the freedom to explore and for me to refuse line when I thought there might be trouble below. I've refused line a couple of times in this conversation, but I've loved watching it go out too and hearing where you've been.

Keep asking. There's lots going on for me.

Brad:

Okay, so what's going on for you?

Sean:

Ha. I didn't mean right now. Like I said, my confidence is growing and I think it's because I find myself drawn into the very kind of life that we are talking about as we discuss. What you can't see is the contented smile on my face. There's this sideline dialogue that's happening with the Spirit and I'm asking lots of things and getting, *ahem*, fairly immediate answers. It's actually kind of humorous really. Most of what I've said in resistance (and not) has come out of an extended time of Listening Prayer.

Brad:

Brilliant! *What if...* what if the growing confidence and the fairly immediate answers are not coincidental? What if they are directly proportional? What if that's how it works? Sure, this is normal. What if it's normative? How would you know it isn't? The unique grace when I pray with a new believer who hears immediately may be that they largely borrow my confidence.

Sean:

Well, here's the thing: I find that the more my confidence grows in Listening Prayer, the less I care about getting the immediate answer. It's not that I am giving up on asking and listening. On the contrary, this has only steadily increased.

And it's not as though I don't get immediate answers. They're actually coming with greater frequency these days. I think it's just that I'm content to wait for an answer and even dwell on the answer a bit when it comes, because I have come to see that Jesus is in fact alive and that he is good. This has changed everything for me. It's the simplest thing but also the most profound. As Christians, it's quite easy to live as though God is not alive and that he is not good. Been there. It's also possible to live as though God is alive and is good but with little or no confidence. Been there too. In a sense, I continue to live in these situations. But I've been asking and listening and helping others to do the same and God's been showing up and, well, it's interesting how everything in life gets transformed when you've got eyes and ears for the Lord's appearing.

Brad:

This is wonderful. The lack of angst around it is wonderful. The angst around listening seems to me to be rooted in that lie about needing to come up with something. I only need to listen. And God doesn't need to do anything (so no presuming). But he's the type of Father who will. If I hear I hear. If not, I'm at peace in his silent presence. This peace helps me hear better.

Sean:

Yes.

Afterword
Brad Jersak

At the end of the day, and of this booklet, those who would practice Listening Prayer and tune in to the living God will, like us, need to let go of preconceived notions that force the spiritual senses into narrow channels. Of course, we all have a tendency to circle around what is familiar and predictable, but the fact of the matter is that hearing and seeing in the life of Listening Prayer cannot be reduced to a single techonology and what we hear and see to a single ideology. Instead we find ourselves open to realities that we could never dream up on our own. With humility and expectancy, we attend closely to the Scriptures, asking ourselves and the Lord Jesus, "What if this were true?":

> [Jesus said,] "I have *many more things to say to you,* but you cannot bear them now. But when He, the Spirit of truth, comes, *He will guide you into all the truth;* for He will not speak on His own initiative, but *whatever He hears, He will speak; and He will disclose to you what is to come.* He will glorify Me, for He will take of Mine and will *disclose it to you.* All things that the Father has are Mine; therefore I said that *He takes of Mine and will disclose it to you"* (John 16:12-15 NASB, *emphasis mine*).

Jesus was quite serious about these promises and he intends

them for us today, but of course this fact alone does not make it any less difficult to know how to proceed. The important thing is simply to enter in at his invitation and become responsive to the living God. There will be disagreements about how the Spirit continues to speak and how we ought to listen. But we must continue enquiring of him and watching for the fruit of listening/obeying. As we share testimonies of the results, let us continue to test and nuance one another in love, even as Agora has tried to model herein.

Appendix 1
"Lining Up"

Brad:

I've been reflecting more on what "lining up with Scripture" means. I like David's simple "Scripture testifies to my testimony" and have also been thinking about Sean's caveats about it not being direct one to one correspondence. I wondered if we could pick up on this a little more because "lining up" is thrown around so much... everywhere from BCS's theme motto verse to the Anglican debates on gay marriage. A shorter term for *lining up with Scripture* is the overused *biblical*... whatever that turns out to mean. There's a difference though.

For some, *biblical* means "it's in the Bible" (contained in the box). But *lining up* might include that which is not in the Bible but consistent with the teachings and trajectory of the Bible (the plumbline).

To my mind, Peter's use of Joel in Acts 2 is an interesting attempt to line up in David's sense of Scripture testifying to my testimony with his "this is that" phrase, which certainly sounds like a one-to-one correspondence but in context, is quite a stretch.

So too, in Acts 15:15, James says at the council in Jerusalem, "The words of the prophets are in agreement with this."

My interest is in the legitimate uses of this method. What is the appropriate use of intermingling testimony and Scripture?

Sean:

I would prefer harmonization rather than lining up. Lining up suggests that Scripture is flatly singular rather than richly plural in expression.

Brad:

Harmonizing... very nice. Scripture plays a C and an E. I play a G. G is not in the Bible. But it is in harmony with the Bible (at the risk of being charged with "extra-biblical revelation").

Sean:

Yes. A different note is inevitable unless we are merely repeating what has been said. The important thing is that the different note chimes with Scripture.

David:

Can we choose another musical term? Harmonization smacks of an imposed consistency, deleting the parts that don't fit... cheap, electronic, synthesizers.

Kevin:

Really? I think of a choir.

Harmonies of different parts around the same melody,

growing in richness with each added voice, even the same parts have different voices... new textures. The goal is not to imitate the melody... first thing you learn in choir. I'm thinking about the Hallelujah Chorus... sometimes I sing it to my daughter (it's amazing what comes out of you when you sing to a five-month-old all the time) and of course it sounds funny and lame no matter how hard I try to texturize my voice. It was written for the harmonies of a choir...

Perhaps Scripture shares that designation... a melody designed to inspire harmonies... That's a beautiful thought really, that God intends for our voices... our textures to get involved.

Indeed, when we hear imitations with no harmonies, singing the melody alone and claiming to be complete, it sounds funny and lame... the melody may be there, but something's missing.

Perhaps it's the postmodern glasses I sport but the idea of something being *lined up* and yet flat resonates with the way I feel about a lot of the single voice songs I hear from within the church... I find myself thinking, "Well, that's not incorrect...BUT..."

David:

I'm happy with your description of harmony. It's just that harmonization makes me think of the kind of harmonization of Scripture that attempts to make everything line up and say the same thing.

Andre:

But when we ultimately see the big picture, everything will line up, won't it? The end of Creation is harmony?

Sean:

Unity rather than uniformity.

Glenn:

David, I know what you are referring to… and I wonder if it isn't a misappropriation of the term, harmonization. The Gospels as they exist are harmonious. But once you put them on the same line, you've flattened the harmony into a distortion of the melody. And it's what I'm referring to above about the difference between seeing and hearing… Only a trained eye can read harmony.

Sam:

We could think of

- Jazz: unpredictable harmonies
- Southern Gospel: some groups are known for their "tight harmonies."
- Heavy Metal: distorted harmony.

These all "fit"!

Appendix 2 - *Mysticeti Discernment* by Brad Jersak

When it comes to discernment, we are and should be like the *Mysticeti.* Who or what are the *Mysticeti*? Some sort of mystical magi? Not at all... that's just the technical name for our friends, the baleen whales. I believe that with those great baleen strainers of theirs, they have the corner on discernment and we might learn from them.

They do not swim around looking for a particular fish to bite, hoping that they don't accidentally get something yucky in their mouths. And neither do we, really. Life doesn't work that way. You can't pick up a *Time* magazine and only read good news or turn on a television and only see good pictures or go into town and only expose yourself to good sights. Every time you read, look, experience... everything in the magazine, movie, ads, and on the streets, in the malls, etc. enters your ears and eyes and senses... i.e. the whale opens its mouth and it all goes in. In fact, when a whale wants to eat, it doesn't just open its mouth... it dives to the ocean bottom, opens wide, and scoops gargantuan amounts of water, shrimp, mud, fish, sticks, weeds into its mouth... We do this from morning until night just by living in the world, leaving our house, engaging with people. Then the whale begins to push everything back out of its mouth, straining it through the baleen apparatus: the strainer doesn't keep bad stuff out... it PUSHES bad stuff out while keeping even the most microscopic bits of nourishment... and it keeps so MUCH krill, plankton, shrimp, etc. that these meals can nourish and grow the greatest mammal in history. From somewhere on the internet (http://www.enchantedlearning.com/subjects/ whales/glossary/indexi-m.shtml):

> *Baleen whales (also known as Mysticeti, or mustached whales) are filter feeders that have baleen, a sieve-like device use for filter feeding krill, copepods, plankton, and small fish. They are the largest whales and have two blowholes. Baleen whales include blue, gray, humpback, minke, bowhead, and right whales. Many baleen whales species are endangered.*

What we have here is not "garbage in, garbage out," but rather, "everything in, garbage out" with an understanding that even the whales develop a sense of where the best feeding routes are and that it's wise to avoid oil slicks. As my friend, Colleen Taylor, wrote in a recent email:

> I don't think "everything in" works if you're going to include ENTERING places like the porn store as a potential source of nourishment. However, walking by the porn store is another matter and fairly unavoidable. Of course there are people who are CALLED to enter porn stores, red light districts, etc., looking for Christ the way Mother Teresa did. Does that mean it is okay for everyone to go there? Does everyone have the same spiritual baleen capacity to sift and spit? No. Even that is part of the discernment process.

The question is what our own spiritual baleen consists of and how effective it is. But the big point here is that you don't strain by not eating for fear of getting something bad. Rather, we take it in and then begin to sift outwards, holding on to the good (as per 1 Thessalonians 5).

This reminds me of the spiritual exercise that I tried for myself: trying to discern my way through the Nag Hammadi Library (the famous Gnostic collection). Some won't read the library for fear of getting mud in their mouth. Others just scan it looking for every error (as some do with my books). But the baleen whale type of Christian is straining for nourishment... what is the truth here? What seems like delicious? What is only edible? What is poisonous? As I read the library, I encountered a spectrum of writers ranging from Spirit-filled to delusional. I found that with God's help and sound mind, one could distinguish small-r revelation from capital-H heresy.

I also noticed this perspective alter my approach to preachers: instead of waiting to pounce on the two or three little errors that I supposed I was hearing (and needed to protect others from believing), I changed my question to, "What did God say through this messenger?" I was straining for truth, not error, and it helped me to hear others, engage others, and sometimes win others just by hearing the truth in them. This is why I can enjoy (without swallowing everything), not only the Gospel of Thomas, but the Gospel of Sri Ramakrishna... which is the same process that Solomon used in compiling the Proverbs. He allowed himself to strain other streams, cultures, and even religions for truth and included the "best of" in his collection... a collection now recognized as Scripture. Yet he was not regarded as a syncretist because he knew that Truth and Wisdom are sourced in God and he endeavored (with varying success) to spit out the rest. With God's Spirit as our reliable Guide into all truth (John 16), so might we.

Authors' Bio Page

Sean Davidson (Ph.D. Cand. McMaster Univ.) specializes in early modern literature. He is Asst. Prof. of English Literature and Interdisciplinary Studies at BCS.

Brad Jersak is a pastor and teacher at Fresh Wind Christian Fellowship. He and his wife, Eden, write books and lead seminars on Listening Prayer.

Sam Berg (D.Min.) is a narrative therapist and is the Professor of Marriage and Family Counseling at BCS.

Dwight Friesen (Ph.D. Cand.) is studying media and theology at the University of Edinburgh. He has also been a pastor, photographer, and graphic designer.

Kevin Hall primarily works and serves in the areas marketing and development in both ministry and business contexts; currently in Port Moody, BC.

Andre Harden is an award winning screenwriter and playwright. He and his family live on Bowen Island, BC where he is developing several feature films and a television series.

David Miller (Ph.D. McMaster Univ.) is Asst. Prof. of New Testament at BCS. His research has focused on early Jewish and Christian beliefs about prophets.

Glenn Runnalls has served at Briercrest for twenty-plus years. Currently he is V.P. of Student Development. He watches Pop Culture and enjoys international cooking.

Colleen Taylor is an educator who is finishing her term as Dean of Student Households at BCS. She is pursuing her career as a singer/songwriter and hopes to live in China some day.

New From Fresh Wind Press

Kissing the Leper:
Seeing Jesus in the Least of These
by Brad Jersak

Jesus once counseled us to "Buy medicine for your eyes from me so you can see" (Revelation 3:18). *Kissing the Leper* is about getting our eyes repaired from religious and cultural prejudice so that we can see Jesus in others, especially those that our world discards as "the least." The author has compiled the voices practitioners to develop a devotional theology of encounter. He challenges us to meet and welcome Christ in human form from society's margins to the banqueting table of God.

From the foreword by Eugene H. Peterson:

Brad Jersak's book is a gathering of field notes on Jesus-sightings among the disabled, the children, the prodigals, and the poor. He has a practiced and discerning eye and ear for bringing Jesus to notice among "the least of these" among whom Jesus is present to be fed and welcomed and clothed and cared for and visited. This is first-hand witness, a freshly articulated documentary, on Jesus' story of the sheep and goats (Matthew 25)—with an emphasis on the sheep who served Jesus when they didn't know they were serving him.

www.freshwindpress.com